Not One Sparrow is Forgotten

Volume II

Not One Sparrow is Forgotten

Volume II

A Weekly Poem to Build Faith in Christ

ERIC D. BENTLEY

RESOURCE *Publications* · Eugene, Oregon

NOT ONE SPARROW IS FORGOTTEN, VOLUME II
A Weekly Poem to Build Faith in Christ

Resource Publications
An Imprint of Wipf and Stock Publishers
199 W. 8th Ave., Suite 3
Eugene, OR 97401

www.wipfandstock.com

PAPERBACK ISBN: 979-8-3852-2663-4
HARDCOVER ISBN: 979-8-3852-2664-1
EBOOK ISBN: 979-8-3852-2665-8

VERSION NUMBER 08/02/24

Contents

Week 1—January 1-7

**Not One Sparrow is Forgotten
(Part One)**

As I was guarding the King's flocks I heard the Lord say to me
"Today is the day when miraculous things you will see
And if you trust me and do each thing that I say
I will convert the King and he will find his way"

So as I finished hearing these words in my head
I saw the King's servants feared they'd be dead
Because the robbers came and scattered the herd
And they vanished before they could say a word

As I think and ponder exactly what I should do
I was shown a blueprint of the next thing to pursue
So as we gathered the sheep and I fought the robbers alone
The Lord's power came over me as each step I was shown

And when the King's servants told him what they had seen
They immediately commanded that I should come unto the King
And the most amazing thing was about to take place
When the King heard my testimony with hope on his face

Alma 17:27–39

Week 2—January 8–14

**Not One Sparrow is Forgotten
(Part Two)**

I woke up one morning and heard the birds start to sing
As one of my servants said, "It's a great day to be the King!"
But there's something people just don't know about me
I feel tormented inside and I never feel free

How could a King who seems to have everything
Just wish that I would drown in the depths of the sea?
So I somehow find strength as I look up in the air
To say these words, "Help me if You are really there."

Then my servants say, "There's something you need to hear
There's a man who has godly strength and no fear."
And as this man was brought before my eyes
I heard him say something to my great surprise
He said, "The Lord asked me to let you know
You are not forgotten, nor is a single sparrow."

And as I ponder these words that were said
A burst of hope starts to fill my empty head
And as my darkness turns into glorious light
My Lord and Savior comes into my sight.

Alma 18:1–41

Week 3—January 15–21

Come What May

It has been a while since I was asked by Him
To baptize the one without blemish or sin
And behind prison walls and around sinful behavior
I try to bring my focus on my loving Savior

The prison guards are mocking and scourging me
And they keep asking me to deny Christ the King
But there's something they don't know about me
I've never been one who could be rattled easily

Most importantly they just don't seem to understand
That I have had many witnesses that Christ is more than a man
So regardless of what happens to me in this prison cell
I'll shout "come what may!" and my soul will be well

Mark 6:17–29

Week 4—January 22–28

Proclaim to the World

As I walk up to the temple my mind drifts away
When I dropped my net for the Lord on that day
I think of walking out to Him on the raging sea
And I remember He taught me, "Keep your eyes fixed on me."

My mind drifts back to when I said with a nod
"Thou art the Christ the living Son of the living God."
Then I remember falling to my knees and bowing my head
As I watched him raise a man back from the dead

These memories keep playing so rapidly in my mind
Of the many times He was so powerful and kind
I'm astonished as I reflect on all of His power
And then I see a lame man holding a single flower

As the man reached his hand out in the midday Sun
I tell him "Of silver and gold I have none."
But the Spirit whispers to me that his faith has been revealed
So I say unto him, "In the name of Jesus of Nazareth you are healed"

And as I see the man leaping and praising the Lord God
I look over to James and John and give them a nod
And tell them "Let's go on as we cannot waste an hour
To show the world of His grace and power."

Acts 3:1–11

Week 5—January 29th—Feb 4th

Your Majestic Hands

I am in awe at the detail in the work of thy Hands
From the cliffs by the ocean to the green prairie lands
Each lily arrayed in glory shining in the sun
Are fingerprints of The Master and Holy One

As I look out at the mountains rising so high
And see the white capped rivers go floating by
I think of when Your hands formed the Earth so long ago
As You prepared it with love so we could develop and grow

But the most amazing work was about to begin
When You created our bodies from our eyes to our skin
In God's image You formed us and took delicate care
To create our hearts and lungs and our fingers and hair

And when I think back on Your amazing creation
I am humbled to think the One who heals nations
Would provide me such an amazing opportunity
To progress on this Earth and return home to Thee.

Genesis 1:1–31

Week 6—February 5–11

Rekindle My Faith

I still remember it like it was only yesterday
When I touched His robe and was healed in every way
But as decades of more challenges have gone by
The pain brings me to my knees and I begin to cry

I have had more sickness and struggles and pain
And felt terrible today as I walked in the rain
So as I lay here at night and reflect on my day
I start to have doubts and it is difficult to pray

I wonder if my faith that was once so very strong
Has started to weaken and has brought my sickness on
As I find the courage to pray I hear You proclaim
"I've felt every sickness and every twinge of your pain
Your faith is still as strong from your head to your toe
And has brought you further than you could possibly know
So continue with your faith each and every day
And be an example to those who haven't found their way."

Mark 5:24–34

Week 7—February 12–18

I Choose You

Out of all the amazing things You've given me
One of the greatest gifts of all is my agency
Since our first parents and on through today
You never compelled me to follow Your way

You provide commandments, scriptures, and oversight
That light the way for me like a full moon at night
But it is up to me to choose the path I will go on
As I choose which foundation to build my house upon

Not only do You know the best path for me
You traveled my path in Gethsemane
So no matter what happens or what this world can do
I can say with all my heart that I will always choose You

2 Nephi 2:27

Courage to Leave

I find myself at a party with music blaring so loud
And as laughter turns to mocking, I don't feel so proud
As I look around the room and wonder just what I've done
I see activities around me that make me want to run

So as I ponder in my mind exactly what I should do
I think of a time when a future prophet turned to You
When he found himself carrying out the orders of a wicked king
Until a courageous man came and prophesied everything

He taught about Your glory from high up above
and taught them to repent so they can feel Your love

And as the future prophet pondered exactly what to do
He ran out of the King's court so He could quickly find You
And all the remaining time of this prophet's days
He preached Your word and was faithful in each way

So now I know it's time for me to make a quick decision
And I see the path I need to take like it's in a vision
And as I leave the party I feel a very powerful thing
I feel as strong as a prophet who ran from a wicked king

Mosiah 17:1–4

Week 9—February 26th—March 4th

Pull the Cord

I had this dream that I remember so well
Of a group of people that jumped out and fell
Straight from the side of their plane in the air
Then they fell toward earth as they looked down in despair

They glanced at each other and all thought the same
"Maybe we can flap our arms and we will be okay?"
But the more they flapped the more they could tell
It did absolutely nothing and so they still fell

So they spread their arms and legs with all their might
But the ground only kept coming closer in sight
Then one of them looked over to another's back
And noticed a glorious parachute was packed

So he shouted "The Lord did something for you and me
He has taken on the sins of the world to set us free
And all we have to do is pull this rip cord at any time
And we'll float down to the ground and will be just fine."

So he pulled the cord and everyone looked on in wonder
As he floated in the air and the rest fell quickly under
Then I looked and beheld my Savior was within reach
And He looked peacefully at me and began to teach

"Each time you sin it's like you are jumping out of a plane
And pulling the rip cord is like repenting in my name
And each of those who will believe and repent
Will draw upon the mercy for which I was sent."

2 Nephi 2:26–27

Week 10—March 5–11

Justice and Mercy

The jury came back and the verdict is in
I have been found guilty of reckless sin
The judge moves the case to the punishment phase
Where my fate will be determined over the next couple days

At night I kneel down in my cold prison cell
And beg for forgiveness as I break down and tell
Of my deep regret as I'm the only one to blame
For my actions that brought this sorrow and shame

And then Christ walked in and opened the prison door
And said to me, "You don't need to suffer for that anymore
I paid for your sin and I suffered your loss
On the day in the garden and up on the cross."

Then my burdens were lifted and I can live to tell
How the Lord set me free from my prison cell
And how He did something so glorious for me
Instead of facing justice I was provided mercy

Alma 42:15

Week 11—March 12–18

Like the Rising Sun

One day as I was praying to the Father above
I expressed my complete admiration and love
And as I kneeled down with my hands against my face
I felt myself being whisked away to a very high place

Then an angel of the Lord came and told me
He could show me anything I wanted to see
So I asked the angel if I could see each occasion
When the Lord helped me through a difficult situation

So I watched on the screen and saw each time
He walked in with me to school to make sure I was fine
Then as I looked over I was so amazed to see
During a bad breakup He was right there with me

Each memory came and went so very fast
As I saw His hand in everything from my past
From the time I was in darkness and found His light
To the time I held my baby all through the night

I realize that no matter what time of night or day
The Lord is simply there for me and won't walk away
So when life gets me down I'll turn to The One
Whose love is dependable as the rising Sun

1 Nephi 10:18

Week 12—March 19–25

Forgiveness is Key

I find myself with my brothers and it's hard to see
How I can act like it's fine that they abandoned me
I can't help but think of when I was sold into Egypt
As I found myself at the bottom of a miserable pit

How can I forgive them for what they've done to me?
How can I just let go of all my pain and grief?
And just then Your sweet words come into my head
And I feel like I have been raised from the dead
"When you discover forgiveness that's where you will see
That through this process is where you will find Me
For unto each and every person I will tell you the same
Your burdens are lifted when you forgive others in my name."

So with love in my heart and a tear in my eye
I tell my brothers I forgive them and I watch them cry
And then a warm feeling comes directly over me
As I feel that forgiveness has now set my soul free.

Genesis 45:1–15

Week 13—March 26th—April 1st

Today is the Day

I have had a life filled with many worldly things
From golden bracelets to diamond rings
But now that I see life through a lens that is wide
I start to realize why I feel so empty inside

It goes back to something that happened long ago
When I was young and thought I knew all there is to know
And I approached Jesus and asked Him what I can do
To obtain eternal life when my time on earth is through

But as He taught I just couldn't seem to see
That He was asking me to stop looking inwardly

And although I can't change things from my past
I can begin to live each day like it's my last
So I gather all my things and walk out my front door
And decide that it's time to give it all to the poor

I then walk into the temple and a peaceful feeling washes over me
As I repent of my sins and feel that I'm finally clean

Mathew 19:16–22

Week 14—April 2–8

Spiritual Personal Trainer

One time I finished my workout and was just so sure
That I signed up for the very best personal trainer
Just when I thought my hardest workout was through
He pushed me beyond what I thought I could do

On days when I texted him to say I really don't care
He responded, "Go to the gym and I'll meet you there."
I realized that without my trainer I would be
Left on my own as a weaker version of me

So I pull into my garage and walk inside my home
And I suddenly realize that I am utterly alone
My wife died years ago and the kids have moved away
And I'm starting to wonder if I can make it another day

And then it hits me the Lord is doing something just for me
Because I didn't sign up for Earth to have it be easy
And as I struggle through my grief and all of my pain
He stands right next to me and says, "I'll help you obtain
The very best version of yourself so you will be
On the road back to your eternal destiny."

Then I get down on my knees and look up to the skies
And I thank You for my struggles with tears in my eyes
For I know that without trials I will never see
You help me become the best version of me.

Ether 12:27

Week 15—April 9–15

Set Me Free

It just seems to be so hard for others to see
That I sometimes feel there's a different person inside of me
I try to do everything that I possibly can
But something flicks a switch inside this broken man

So one day as I stood with the chains that were on me
I heard the voice of my Shepherd who came to set me free
And as Christ looked in my soul and saw my true self inside
He blessed me and I finally felt the real me come alive

I don't know why it was time for His grace to send
Healing to my suffering that seemed to have no end
But from this day forward I plan to do everything that I can
To sing the praises of my Lord to any fellow man

Luke 8:26–36

Week 16—April 16–22

Out of the Boat Again

As we fish in Galilee on a quiet spring night
It turns to morning without a single fish in sight
And I think back on the day I swallowed my pride
When the Savior said to cast my net to the other side

I remember that day and I quickly feel calm
As I remember hundreds of fish passing through each palm
And on that day I dropped my net in front of Him
As I confessed I have lived a life filled with sin

But He said to me with a peaceful look on His face
"You are forgiven my child but you must go with haste
So come with Me and do all that you can
To follow Me and become a fisher of man."

And now that I come out of this precious memory
I see the resurrected Savior at the edge of the sea
And with a glow on His face and a twinkle in his eye
His familiar voice says, "Cast your net to the right."

And as James and John pull in the biggest catch ever
I dive in headfirst and swim straight to my Savior

John 21:3–7

Week 17—April 23–29

The Centurion

I have been a Centurion nearly my entire life
And I have guarded these lands through chaos and strife
But I thought the easiest way to deal with what I see
Was to harden my heart and become numb to everything

Then day after day I saw a man named Jesus go throughout
And show kindness and mercy as He taught what life's about
I've never really felt anything like this before
As I've see with Him there is never a closed door

Then one day as I was making my daily rounds
One of my soldiers came sprinting through town
And he said my captain had fallen sick again
But there's not enough time say goodbyes to him

Then I looked up and saw Jesus walking towards me
And I knew He had the power if I could just believe
So I bowed down and said "Knowing what I've seen and I heard
I know You can heal my captain if You will just say the word."

Then Jesus looked right at me and to my great surprise
He said He has not seen such faith as He looked me in the eyes
And as I sprinted home to see my captain's relieved face
I realized I had just experienced the Son of God's grace.

Mathew 8:5–13

Week 18—April 30th—May 6th

Suffer the Children to Come Unto Me

I remember back when I was just a young boy
When there was a time I felt total peace and joy
It was when Jesus was teaching those around Him
How to be more loving and how to repent of their sin

As I put my ear to the door I could begin to hear
His voice of love that instantly calmed my fears
So without hesitation and when He was right in my sight
I ran straight to the Lord and hugged Him with all my might

Then the rulers and teachers tried to send me and my friends away
Until the Lord said, "Suffer the Children to come unto me today
For the Kingdom of Heaven is likened unto these children
And unless you have simple faith like them you will not be let in."

Years later I still think back on that wonderful day
And know the key is to still run to Him in every way
For I know that my soul will never suffer any harm
If I stay held in His strong and mighty arms.

Luke 18:15–17

My Mother Knew It

As I read about the young warriors who had no fear
Because they believed what their mothers taught so dear
My mind drifts back to a different place and time
Where I treasured the words I was taught by mine

I can still remember the sound of my Mother's gentle voice
As she taught me how I could make every choice
She taught me of the people and prophets of old
Who showed how to have faith in Christ and be bold

Because they could garner strength from the Holy One
Who will never leave their side even after the battle is won
I can still remember the faithful look in her eyes
As she taught me of the everlasting power of Christ

So as I go into different types of battles each day
I'll remember if I don't doubt He will prepare a way
And even when I have days where I am taking hit after hit
I'll know the Lord will help me and my Mother knew it

Alma 56:47–48

Week 20—May 14–20

My Burdens Were Lifted

One day I woke up and just didn't feel the same
It was like a pile of bricks on my back as I felt my shame
I was racked by the thought of my decisions and sin
And started to wonder if I could find my way again

So I packed up my hunting gear and went away
Hoping it would make me feel better today
And as I got deep in the woods a thought came to my mind
Of my Father who taught me of the Savior of Mankind

His words came back to me as if he was out here with me
That repentance is the key to our salvation for eternity
So I kneeled down in the woods and repented of my sins
And I suddenly felt the Lord's light from within

Then that load of bricks that was weighing down on me
Was lifted from my back and I felt glorious and free.

Enos 1:1–8

Week 21—May 21–27

On the Winning Team

One time I had the most amazing dream
I dreamed we were lined up to be picked for a team
And as I looked across the way that is when I beheld
There were names that were called out to one side of the field

Abraham, Issac, and Jacob were called aloud
And as they ran on the field the crowd cheered so proud
Then I heard many other names called out on that day
And I watched in disbelief as they ran the other way

But then I heard my name called out so very clear
And I ran out onto the field without a doubt or fear
Then I looked up and to my great surprise
The Savior was standing in front of my eyes

And He looked at me and said with a peaceful smile
"I have chosen You for my team and I'll be with you all the while."

Abraham 3:22–28

Week 22—May 28th—June 3rd

More With Us Than Them

One time I was having a very rough day
Because I was in a battle from every which way
I turned my head and just to the right of me
A group was mocking those who believe in Thee

Then I looked over and heard loud ridiculing voices
Taunting those of us who were making righteous choices
But the worst was when those who used to be my ally
Turned their back on me and so I started to cry

But then I heard Your gentle voice that touched my soul
Say "Turn around as there's something you should know
There's a legion of my angels who will always be around you
To bear you up as you seek me in all that you do."

2 Kings 6:15–17

Week 23—June 4–10

Faith in the Ark

As I walk down the rows of this ark while on the sea
I can't help but stop for a minute and wonder what will be
I feel each wave move this ark up and down in the water
As I walk around the huge ark with my daughter

But while we are safe I just can't get out of my mind
The lives of those who were lost because they seemed blind
As they thought that I must have gone insane
When I begged them to get in the ark in the rain

So as I have no idea how long this ark will sail
I confidently know in the Lord's hands I will be well
Because the Lord always comes through in the nick of time
When we have faith in His power knowing our souls will be fine.

Genesis 7:15–19

Week 24—June 11–17

Hold to the Iron Rod

One day I was driving with my girlfriend by an empty home
And I said it's getting late as I saw the time on my phone

But with her inquisitive eyes she said she wanted to go in
And see what we could find in a place we've never been

Like the great and spacious building floating up in the air
I know that I really shouldn't go inside of there
But the next thing I know I turn around the car
And I say let's just go in a little but not too far

As I feel myself walking across the deadened sod
To my amazement I saw an imaginary iron rod
Extending on a path directly back to my car
And continuing on to her house that wasn't very far

So I tell her I really don't think this is a good idea today
And with the strength of the Lord I turn and walk away
And on my way back home after dropping her off that night
I praise the Good Shepherd for shining His light

1 Nephi 15:23–24

Week 25—June 18-24

Never Another Doubt

One day when I was fishing with my son out on the sea
He told me that there's something that is hard to believe
How Jesus could take on all of our sins and pain
And know each of us like He is seeing it again

My son said it's just hard to believe something is true
Unless he can see it and analyze it through and through

Then I leaned down to my son and I said with a smile
"I've been in those same shoes and have even walked a mile
But the day I touched the Savior's scarred hands and side
It was like there was an instant shifting of the tide
When the resurrected Lord proclaimed unto me
"Blessed more is he who doesn't see yet still believes"

So I turned to my son and said "It's okay to have doubts
In fact that's an important part of what this life's all about.
But if you can put yourself out there and choose faith over fear
You will soar to heights where your mind will be clear
And after this trial of your faith the Lord will reveal unto you
Everything you need like He's standing in front of you."

John 20:26–29

Week 26—June 25th—July 1st

Protection for the Soul

One time a chess lesson was being taught to me
And my teacher taught me how to guard the King
He taught me that I should build a wall around him
So the other side could not attack and get in

Then I realized the Lord has taught the same thing to me
He has taught me how to build a wall of safety
As each scripture I read and prayer that I say
Will protect my soul each and every day

So I'll keep my covenants and look up and see
The walls of safety as they are built up for me
And I'll thank the Lord for giving me power to endure
And find protection to my soul as I remain true and pure

1 Nephi 15:24

Week 27—July 2-8

Yoked with the Savior

Today I was prompted to perform a difficult task
And it's the kind of thing that I really want to ask
Are You sure this is what You want me to do?
Is there perhaps someone else who could do this for You?

But as I humble myself and think about it more
I am reminded of a sermon You gave by the shore
When You said to take Your yoke upon us and fight the fight
Because when we are yoked with You our burdens will be light

And I stop for a moment and am sorry that I ever wonder
Whether I'll be okay in the hands of He who commands thunder
So as I go back to this task that You have asked of me
I triumphantly proclaim "I will do anything for Thee!"

Mathew 11:28–30

Week 28—July 9–15

Gratitude During the Storm

As I'm tied up on this ship and the waves are coming in
I start to reflect on what we've done and where we've been
I think of how many revelations my brothers have had
And I am having a difficult time not being incredibly mad

Because now it seems they have finally figured out a way
To wreck our ship and have today be our last day
But as I think back on the wonders that I have seen
I know that the Lord will never abandon me

So as our ship tosses around like a cork on the sea
I stop and give a prayer of thanks unto Thee
For all of Your patience and all of Your love
That has shown me You're watching from above

And in a shocking and sudden turn of events
My brothers untie me and the viscous storm relents
So I move my sore neck and look up into the air
And praise my Lord and Savior for always being there.

1 Nephi 18:8–23

Week 29—July 16-22

Faith that Can't be Wrecked

It has not been long since You changed my name
And my outlook on life would never be the same
So as my ship wrecks and I swim for shore
I realize that I don't need to worry any more

As I work diligently to get pieces of wood from the sand
A giant viper strikes towards me and latches on my hand
I don't even stop to think this might be dire
As I shake the viper off right into the fire

Then I look around and am startled to see
The shocked looks on their faces as they stare at me
But the greatest thing was yet to be revealed
When a crowd of people faithfully ask to be healed

I'm in awe at the relentless nature of God's Son
Who leaves the ninety and nine to go after the one
So I look up to the heavens that are up above
And praise the Lord for His mercy and love

Acts 28:1-9

Week 30—July 23-29

Getting My Own Answer

I'll never forget the look my father had on his face
When he gathered us and said we need to leave this place
Before we packed our things and headed out on our way
I looked out across the city and wanted to stay

Even though my father told me all the Lord had said
There was turmoil that kept beating like a drum in my head
So that night I got next to my bed to kneel
And asked the Lord if I could begin to feel
What my Father felt when he heard the Lord's voice
So I too would know that we needed to make this choice

And like a beacon that shines in a dark night
The Lord helped me know it was time to take our flight
Into the wilderness so that our family could be
Protected by the everlasting Lord who loves me.

1 Nephi 2:16

Week 31—July 30th—August 5th

Leave it all Behind

As I'm on my way back to see my family
I start to reflect on the things that happened to me
As I've tried to be someone the Lord could rely on
To carry out His work and get difficult tasks done

But as I return from the marketplace I feel so alone
As my preaching of repentance was met with stones
And I think how clearly I heard the Lord's voice
Tell me to move my family and I knew there's no choice

So as I walk on this dusty road and wonder what to do
I realize that there is nothing I can't do through You
And my attitude goes from fear to "Thy will be done"
As I decide to turn it over to God's Beloved Son.

1 Nephi 2:1–4

Week 32—August 6–12

The Joy of Repentance

My father is a prophet but I just don't know
Why he seems to bind himself wherever he'll go
Because I think that the very best thing for me
Is to just go around and be wild and free

Then one day as I was out on the town with my friends
An angel of the Lord told me "This is where this road ends
For if you continue to persecute the righteous in town
Your soul will forever be dragged way down
To the one who shackles you with his chains
And who will abandon you in your heartache and pain."

Then as I laid down on the ground as if it was my bed
The teachings of my father began to play in my head
And I suddenly remembered the peaceful look on his face
When he taught me of the Savior's atonement and grace

So I repented and said, "Lord I'll do everything I can
If You can give some more grace to this broken man"
And then the most amazing thing I could ever see
Was when I saw those chains being loosened from me

And my unending grief and the iron fist of pain
Turned to joy like a withered plant that got rain
So starting today I will go and tell everyone I know
How to avoid spiritual death and endless sorrow.

Alma 36:6–24

Week 33—August 13–19

What am I Still Doing Here?

I seem to be the last prophet to tell this sad tale
Of the destruction of my people who fought and fell
Because their pride set in and they forgot the very thing
That gave them each breath and every reason to sing

And as I wander around pondering the next thing I should do
I get discouraged as I thought my mission was through
But I press forward each day wondering why I can't see the vision
Of what the Lord wants as I near the end of this mission

And as I start writing again I realize that it's just so hard for me
To write the words that could be helpful for others to see
So I write about how the difficulty and awkwardness of my hands
Will cause those to mock who will receive it in other lands

And then I hear the comforting words of my Lord
Say "Fools mock but they shall mourn."
And He comforts me and lets me know
That weaknesses are what allow us to grow

And if we can just come unto the Lord in humility
He will turn our weaknesses into strengths for us to see
Because the Savior of the world knows exactly what we need
And if we can just trust in Him He will help us succeed.

Ether 12:23–28

Week 34—August 20–26

Peace Under the Tree

I have worked all my days through grief and pain
To sit under the tree of life where I can gain
The feeling of peace from the Lord above
As I taste of His fruit and feel of His love

It hasn't been the most direct route here
But I can honestly say I finally have no fear
I feel like my weaknesses have been made strong
As my Lord and God tells me that I belong

I see the great and spacious building over in a cloud
And hear their voices that are mocking me so loud
But there's something they don't seem to know about me
In my Savior's arms I feel loved and I'm free

The chains that once shackled me fell to the floor
As my Savior tells me "You don't have to live like this any more."

So with a gentle and subtle shake of my head
I heed them not and focus on my fruit instead
And I look around and tell everyone that I see
To press forward and taste the fruit with me.

1 Nephi 8:10–33

Week 35—August 27th—September 2nd

Let Your Light Shine

Sometimes I feel like I am shackled by these chains
That seem to drag me down through heartache and pain
But it's the decisions of others that has brought me here
And I can't break this cycle so I begin to fear

I want to sound the trumpet like an angel in the night
To let those around me know we cannot lose this fight
Because it seems like some people are just giving in
To the adversary's grip on wickedness and sin

And then I step back and I begin to realize
That it's up to each person whether they want the prize
For following the narrow path the Lord has set forth
As He hands us a compass that points to His North

So I look to The One who can calm all of my fears
And I see Your scarred hand wipe away my sad tears
And then You say something so soft and so gently
"Each person's salvation is between them and me
So do your best to be loving to all you know
And let your light shine the way they should go."

Mathew 5:14–16

Week 36—September 3–9

In Your Time and Your Way

There are times when it's hard to see what's in store
So I humbly kneel down on my bedroom floor
And I seek strength to get through this difficult task
And I wonder when it will end but I'm hesitant to ask

Then I hear Your comforting words say unto me
"Faith is the hope for things that are not seen
Doubt not fear not because it is not yet known
For after the trial of your faith is when you'll be shown"

"For if I show you the end before you believe
It wouldn't be faith it would be a reality
But your faith will allow you to move a mountain
And my power will flow from an eternal fountain."

So I realize the amazing thing You are doing for me
Is teaching me through each trial to believe in Thee
And to know You are with me through all of my pain
And believe this trial will end in Your time and Your way.

Mathew 17:20

Week 37—September 10–16

Warriors for the Lord

Our fathers made an oath with the Lord and without exception
They promised they wouldn't take up a single weapon
For they had hope for a better place and time
When their sons could live in peace and be fine

But as we sit by the fire we see a burden is on their backs
Because the enemy forces are planning their attacks
Our fathers can either break the oath they made unto Thee
Or they can stand up and fight to protect their family

So some of us go into the woods and we kneel and pray
Then we hear Your comforting words as You say
"I know you are young but there's something you must know
As your Mothers have taught I'll be with you where you go
So let your Fathers keep their oaths they made unto me
And I'll arm you with strength this world has never seen."

Alma 53:14–21

Week 38—September 17-23

He Will Remember Them No More

One night I had the most interesting dream
I looked back on my life and it started to seem
Like everything I had ever done or said
Was stored like a computer inside of my head

So I clicked on the first file and immediately could see
That I was not the kind of person I knew I could be
And I clicked on another and to my great surprise
I was acting like a blindfold was in front of my eyes

When I found another bad file I started to shake
And I worried that from this dream I would never wake

Then my Savior walked in and stood before my eyes
And with a smile He reached out as I started to cry
He said, "Don't worry child those sins were forgotten by me
The night you kneeled and asked the Father to forgive thee.

Go forth and try your best to live what's in store
And I the Lord God will remember them no more."

Jeremiah 31:34

Week 39—September 24–30

The Lord Will Provide a Way

My brothers and I have been commanded to obtain
The records that have the history of our name
But after two failed attempts things are looking dim
As two of my brothers just throw the towel in

But I look at them and with confidence in my eye
I tell them I'm going back for another try
And on my way toward the city's great walls
I say a quick prayer and promise to give my all

And as I approach the city I am startled to see
A path to obtain the plates is right before me
Because the Lord blesses those who give all they can
And He will provide them a way to carry out His plan.

1 Nephi 4:1–17

Week 40—October 1–7

Have Faith and Go to Work

When I was young and was with my family
We had to hunt before we made it to the sea
But as I drew back my steel bow that worked so well
I felt it snap into pieces that immediately fell

My brothers were furious and as our hunger grew stronger
My family complained that we couldn't go any longer

As their faith turned to doubt and they continued to cry
I decided it was time for me to go out and try
Anything and everything that I could possibly do
And then have faith that the Lord will come through

So I found the nearest tree and cut part of it to the ground
And started to make a bow until the sun went down
With each carve of my knife and stretch of the string
I gave thanks unto You and I started to sing

And When my bow was finished I heard You say to me
"I need you to strengthen their faith and set them free
Go unto your father and ask him to know
Where you should hunt and there you will go."

So I did exactly what You asked me to do
And for the first time in a while I saw my father pray to You
As he got up from his knees and walked from his tent
He peacefully looked at me as he knew where I should be sent

And after a few hours hunting in the middle of the day
I knew this food would excite them in every way
But the greatest feeling came when You helped me know
It's best to go to work than stay in my sorrow.

1 Nephi 16:18–32

Week 41—October 8–14

Still Small Voice

In this world there are so many loud voices
That try to poke fun at righteous choices
With a flick of the thumb you can find yourself in
A virtual world filled with contention and sin

If you seek contention that is when you will find
Only the adversary wants that state of mind
For his ultimate goal at the end of the day
Is to have you feel miserable in every way

But there is One mightier who stands above all names
Who knows my weaknesses and still loves me the same
And Christ whispers to me in a still and small voice
"You're worth it my child, you can make the right choice."

3 Nephi 11:29–33

Week 42—October 15–21

Loosen the Bands and Forgive

I find myself face down and tied up on a hot day
And there's just nothing I can seem to do or say
That will stop my brothers from carrying out their plan
As they try to put an end to this righteous man

After they left me for dead I know You are the only one
Who can hear my cries as I roast in this hot Sun
So I pray unto the Father with the faith like Moses
Who never doubted even in the wilderness

And as I finish my prayer I look down and see
These bands have suddenly been loosened from me

And as I walk back to my bothers I can hear Your voice
Say "You are about to have a defining choice
You can let this anger build up in your mind
Or you can choose right now to be meek and kind."

So when I got back my brothers fell down on their knees
When I frankly forgave them and turned it over to Thee.

1 Nephi 7:16–21

Week 43—October 22–28

My Spiritual GPS

I sometimes feel like I'm so lost in the crowd
Like I'm gasping for air among those who are loud
And when I think of breaking free I just don't know
If I can bring myself up from this endless sorrow

I start to get confused as I wonder what I should do
And I start to doubt if I can make my way to You
But then I remember a story about a family who was lost
And everything they tried came at such a great cost

Until they realized their compass would not show them the way
Unless they were diligent and had faith in You each day
So I remember my blessing I received when I was young
And my GPS lights my way like the midday Sun

Because I'm shown what You have in store for me
If I can turn my GPS on and move toward Thee

1 Nephi 16:10–16

Week 44—October 29th—November 4th

Peace be Still

Sometimes I wake up and feel numb to the news
Because each day I feel like I'm going to lose
The boisterous noise that blares through the air
Makes me wonder why I should even care

Then I turn off the news and like a lighthouse at night
I look over and see my scriptures radiating with light
So I open them up and flip right open to the page
When You calmed the tempest with the storm in a rage

Your words "peace be still" flow over me like rain
And Your infinite grace starts to replace my pain
So I decided that in the morning I will try something new
Instead of turning on the news I will turn my thoughts to You

Because I know there's nothing I wouldn't do or say
So that I can feel Your peace each and every day.

Mark 4:36–41

Week 45—November 5–11

Stand in Holy Places

I am standing at the edge of egregious sin
And I don't know if I should walk out or stay in
So as I contemplate exactly what I should do
I feel my thoughts move directly to You

I'm reminded of a sermon I heard as a young man
About King David who was strong and had big plans
But who in a moment of weakness stood out and stared
At a woman from his balcony when he shouldn't have been there

And this moment of weakness put him on a path where he would be
Wrapped in sin's chains where he couldn't see the key
A mighty man who had enough faith to slay a giant
Was brought to his knees because he was so defiant

So as I contemplate whether to go in and suffer spiritual loss
Your words flood my mind, "It is far better to take up your cross"
So I walk out quickly and go back to my car
And give thanks to my Savior for all that You are.

Mathew 16:24–26

Week 46—November 12–18

On the Seashore of Faith

I climbed a mountain to find what I should do today
And what You said to me surprised me in every way
You commanded me to build a ship that would take my family
To the promised land across this great sea

I'm so nervous as I know we don't have a single tool
And my brothers look for any chance to call me a fool
I've never built a ship but I've learned something about You
You would never command me to do something I can't do

So when the ship is finished and we launch into the sea
A feeling of peace and calm come washing over me
To help me know that no matter what will come my way
I can get through it if I can trust in You each day.

1 Nephi 17:7–14

Week 47—November 19–25

Switch Points

When I look back on my decisions I start to realize
There was a simple decision right in front of my eyes
There was one path that led me away from Your Love
And there was one path that led me to the Lord above

But when I look back I am very surprised to see
I didn't realize the things that took me away from Thee
Now that I've been forgiven by Your infinite grace
I will never again choose to leave Your embrace

And as I approach decisions all I want to do
Is choose the path that takes me straight to You.

Mathew 12:30

Week 48—November 26th—December 2nd

He Changed My Name

I still remember it like it just happened yesterday
When Your voice shook me as I was on my way
With a heart filled with stone and ice running in my veins
I went out and tried to make others feel the same

But somehow You saw the potential in me
And changed my focus from what I did to what I'll be
And with humility in my heart and with my head bowed low
l knew it was time to turn it over to You and let go

So as You opened my eyes I realize I can now see
That you've always been standing right next to me
And as I go out to preach Your word with my new name
I am determined that my soul will never be the same.

Acts 26:9–18

Week 49—December 3–9

Faith Before Knowledge

I will never forget the best feeling in my life
When I was going through heartache and strife
I just couldn't figure out exactly what to do
Until that glorious day when I saw You

I watched with wonder as Your finger reached with care
And touched the smooth stones that I had brought there
But Your question to me is what amazed me on this day
When You asked me, "Do you believe all I shall say?"

And even without knowing what You would say
I knew for sure You would never lead me astray
So without hesitation I faithfully said unto Thee
"I believe everything Thou will ever say to me!"

And just then I felt an amazing power come to my soul
As what I believe instantly turned into what I know.

Ether 3:1–20

Week 50—December 10–16

He Trusts Me

There were many experiences during our first years
Where I knew He is the Savior and I was brought to tears
Like when the angel said Mary would conceive the Son of God's life
And to not be afraid to take Mary as my wife

I also remember in Bethlehem on that silent night
Watching Jesus born under the star's bright light
And I cannot forget the day everyone stopped what they were doing
When the three wisemen bowed down and worshipped their King

But I think the most powerful feeling happened on a day
When I felt so helpless in every possible way
Mary and I looked at each other in shock and made no sound
As the young Jesus who was in my care could not be found

We searched for three days and it brought me to my knees
To beg the Father for help as I petitioned my nervous pleas
Then I heard a voice that came from the Father above
"Go ye unto the temple where He is ministering in love."

And as Mary and I rushed to the temple we were amazed to see
The young boy Jesus was teaching the doctors with authority
So right then I offered up a prayer in thanks to The One
Who has somehow trusted me to raise His only Son.

Luke 2:40–52

Week 51—December 17–23

Try Your Best, the Lord will do the Rest

As I am nearing the end of my days here on earth
I ponder each memory and all of my worth
I think of the time the Angel Gabriel appeared to me
And told me I would bear the Savior who I would soon see

And I remember asking if I could possibly be the one
Who was preordained to carry God's only Son
And I remember His loving voice at that time
Telling me to do my best and it will all be fine

Then I think back on the wedding feast when I was in a snare
And I looked and beheld my precious Son was right there
And He comforted and helped me know it will be just fine
And we watched in amazement as He turned the water into wine

And now that I know I am nearing the end of my life
I start to feel anxious and feel burdened with strife
But as I look back on the things my Savior has done for me
I realize he has prepared me for all eternity

And His words come back to keep trying my best
And know the Savior will step up and do the rest.

Luke 1:26–38

Week 52—December 24-31

Never Look Back

The more I follow Your light the more I can see
Some of the tactics and traps of the adversary
One of them is to tell me because of my past
I will never measure up and I will finish last

he wants me to dwell on my past sin and pain
And lies to me that things will never change
But the eternal truth comes from my Savior and Redeemer
That I have been cleansed from my sin and my soul is cleaner

Like a chalkboard that had marks from bottom to top
But is now completely erased and has no chalk

These words from my Redeemer come into my mind
That give me perspective so I am no longer blind
"I'm more interested in your future than I am in your past
And I want you to have this feeling that will last
So with your hand to the plow you can boldly say
You will never look back starting today."

Mathew 7:24-27